W9-BVD-446

Little Guides to
Great Lives

NELSON MANDELA

Published in 2018
by Laurence King Publishing Ltd
361–373 City Road
London EC1V 1LR
United Kingdom
Tel: +44 20 7841 6900
Fax: +44 20 7841 6910
E-mail: enquiries@laurenceking.com
www.laurenceking.com

Illustrations © 2018 Hannah Warren

Isabel Thomas has asserted her right under the Copyright,
Design, and Patents Act 1988 to be identified as the
Author of this Work.

All rights reserved. No part of this publication may be
reproduced or transmitted in any form or by any means,
electronic or mechanical, including photocopy, recording,
or any information storage and retrieval system, without
prior permission in writing from the publisher.

A catalog record for this book is available from the
British Library

ISBN: 978-1-78627-195-2

Commissioning Editor: Chloë Pursey
Editor: Katherine Pitt
Design concept: Charlotte Bolton
Designer: The Urban Ant Ltd.

Printed in China

Other *Little Guides to Great Lives*:
Marie Curie
Charles Darwin
Amelia Earhart
Frida Kahlo
Leonardo da Vinci

Little Guides to
Great Lives

NELSON
MANDELA

Written by
Isabel Thomas

Illustrations by
Hannah Warren

Laurence King Publishing

Nelson Rolihlahla Mandela
1918-2013

Nelson Mandela was the first black president of South Africa. His story is extraordinary. It's not just about one person—but a whole country's fight for freedom.

It begins in the tiny South African village where Nelson was born. He grew up surrounded by rolling hills and green valleys. He felt free.

But as he got older, Nelson realized that black South Africans were not really free at all. Only white people were allowed to vote, and have a say in how the country was run. It was dangerous to speak out against this, but Nelson did not let fear stop him. He set out to change the system.

Nelson's parents gave him the <u>Thembu</u> name Rolihlahla. It means "pulling the branch of a tree"—a.k.a. "troublemaker!"

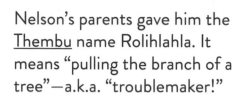

Gadla Henry Mphakanyiswa
Nelson's father, a chief of the Thembu people

Rolihlahla Mandela
Born 18 July 1918

Nosekeni Fanny
Nelson's mother

Nelson's family were important and respected, but this did not mean a life of luxury. They lived in simple huts with mud walls, sleeping on mats without pillows and cooking over a fire pit.

While the men of the village worked away from home in farms or gold mines, the women and children looked after crops and livestock.

When Rolihlahla was five, he began helping his family by herding sheep and goats. In his spare time, he and his friends had adventures in the countryside...

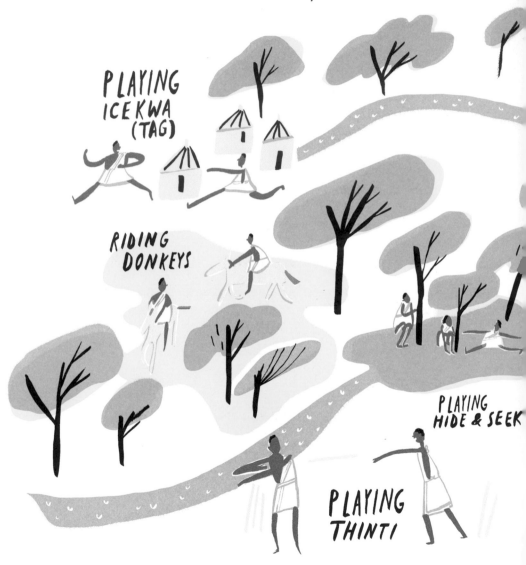

PLAYING
ICE KWA
(TAG)

RIDING
DONKEYS

PLAYING
HIDE & SEEK

PLAYING
THINTI

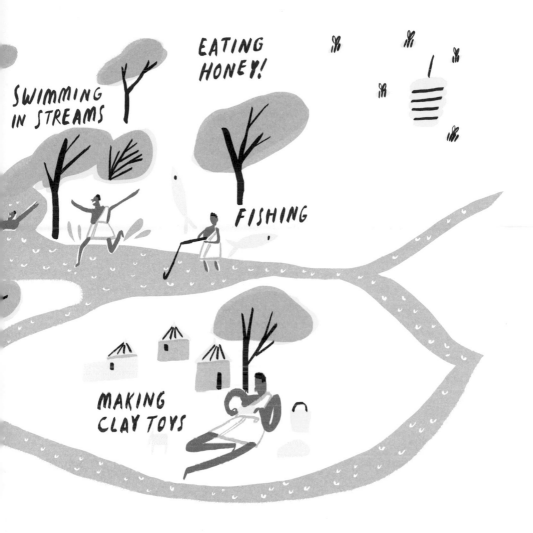

SWIMMING IN STREAMS

EATING HONEY!

FISHING

MAKING CLAY TOYS

How to play thinti
Push two sticks (the targets) into the ground, about
98 feet apart. Split into two teams. Each team has to throw
sticks at the other team's target to try and knock
it down. Try to defend your target and stop the other
team from collecting their sticks!

One day, a family friend suggested that he should go to school. Rolihlahla was proud and excited—no one in his family had been to school before.

The school was run by <u>missionaries</u>, and taught pupils about British ideas and British culture. On the first day, the teacher even gave the children new English names.

Nelson learned about African culture and customs from his family. His mother told him fables about being kind to others. His father told stories of historic battles and warriors. He also learned from his adventures with his friends.

"A donkey once tipped me head first into a thorn bush.

It was so embarrassing!

I learned never to laugh at other people."

Nelson grew up feeling happy and free. But one day, just after his twelfth birthday, his father died. Nelson's life was about to change.

The acting king of the Thembu people offered to give Nelson a new home. The royal household in Mqhekezweni was known as the Great Place. It was not far from the village, but to Nelson it was a different world.

Everything was new and exciting. Uncle Jongi and his wife treated Nelson just like their own son, Justice. The boys became as close as brothers.

Jongintaba Dalindyebo
Acting king of the
Thembu people

Uncle Jongi thought Nelson would make an excellent advisor to future Thembu leaders. He was sent to the best schools to finish his education. Nelson worked hard and did well.

We nicknamed Nelson "Grandpa" because he looked so serious!

He also kept learning from everything he saw around him. The Thembu people often gathered at the Great Place to discuss problems like drought and new laws. Nelson watched the tribal meetings carefully.

Nelson had his own dreams for the future. He wanted to become an interpreter or clerk. These were some of the best jobs a black man could get in South Africa at the time.

He began studying at Fort Hare, South Africa's leading university for black students, where he met his lifelong friend, Oliver Tambo. But his dreams didn't last long.

In his second year, Nelson supported a student <u>protest</u> about the quality of the university's food. He and Oliver were both expelled.

"I knew I needed to compromise, but something inside me would not let me. It was the **hardest decision** I'd ever made—but I felt it was the **right thing** to do."

Back at home in Mqhekezweni, things got even worse. Uncle Jongi was furious and arranged marriages for Nelson and Justice to try and make them settle down. They came up with a secret plot to run away.

In 1941, Nelson and Justice ran away to Johannesburg, South Africa's biggest city. It was known as the Place of Gold. They hoped to get jobs in a gold mine and make new lives.

Their first view of Johannesburg was a maze of glittering lights. Electricity was a luxury in the countryside, and Nelson had never seen so many electric lights in one place.

Nelson and Justice found jobs in a gold mine the next day. But it was clear that only the white mine-owners were rich. The black workers lived in huts and slept in concrete bunks, working long hours for little pay.

Not long after starting, they were summoned to the headman's office. Uncle Jongi had tracked them down, and ordered the headman to send them home at once!

Nelson came up with a new plan that would allow him to stay in Johannesburg. He decided to finish his degree and become a lawyer.

His friend Walter Sisulu helped him find a job as a clerk at a law firm. He worked hard by day, and studied hard in the evenings.

Walter Sisulu
Estate agent & future leader
of the <u>ANC</u>

Nelson lived in Alexandra <u>township</u>. It was an overcrowded and desperately poor area of the city. Homes did not have electricity or running water. But it was one of the only places in South Africa where black Africans could buy their own land. This sense of freedom made Nelson feel at home.

In Johannesburg, Nelson met people from all over South Africa—white and black—who wanted black South Africans to have the same <u>rights</u> as white South Africans.

Some of Nelson's new friends were members of the African National Congress (ANC). The ANC wanted non-white Africans to have the right to vote, rather than being ruled by a whites-only government.

Nelson began going to meetings and found himself getting more involved. He also wanted to change the system.

"why should my life be decided by the color of my skin?"

The ANC had been fighting for freedom for more than 30 years. But the situation for black people seemed to be getting worse, not better.

In 1944, Nelson, Walter Sisulu, and Oliver Tambo set up the <u>ANC Youth League</u>. They wanted to get more supporters and make the government take notice.

Speeches and meetings did not seem to be making a difference. Instead, the ANC Youth League planned to protest by marching through the streets.

Mahatma Gandhi

Nelson was inspired by Mahatma Gandhi. Gandhi was leading peaceful protests in India, to try and end British rule without fighting.

But the more that black people protested, the harder the white government tried to stay in charge. In 1948, a new government was elected with the slogan "the white man must always remain boss."

They introduced a system of laws and rules called <u>apartheid</u>, forcing white and non-white South Africans to live apart.

Black and white people had separate schools, beaches, and churches. They had to use separate buses, drinking fountains, and entrances to offices and shops. A white and a black person could not get married. They could not even share a table in a café or play sport together.

If a black person failed to follow these rules,
they were breaking the law,
and could be sent to prison.

Apartheid was a huge shock, but it made Nelson and his friends feel more determined than ever.

In 1952, the ANC began a peaceful protest called the <u>Defiance Campaign</u>. They risked prison by ignoring the whites-only signs in post offices, shops, and trains.

The campaign spread around South Africa. Over 8,500 people were arrested, including Nelson. They proved they weren't afraid of going to prison for a few days.

The laws did not change, but tens of thousands of new members joined the ANC. It was getting stronger.

The government banned Nelson and the
other ANC leaders from attending
meetings or protesting against apartheid.
But he kept working for them in secret.
The struggle for freedom had become
his life.

Nelson was now a qualified lawyer, and
in 1952 he set up his own law firm
with his friend Oliver Tambo.

It was the only South African law firm run by black lawyers, and the waiting room was always crowded. It was so easy to break the law under apartheid. Thousands of people were being charged with crimes for doing everyday things.

Apartheid laws said that white and non-white people had to live in separate areas. Every week, people came to Nelson and Oliver for help because they were being forced out of their homes.

No matter how good Nelson and Oliver were at their jobs, and no matter how hard the ANC campaigned, they couldn't stop this from happening.

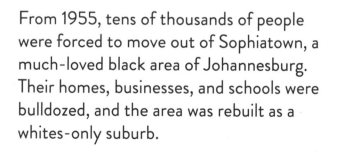

From 1955, tens of thousands of people were forced to move out of Sophiatown, a much-loved black area of Johannesburg. Their homes, businesses, and schools were bulldozed, and the area was rebuilt as a whites-only suburb.

Nelson was beginning to feel that the ANC would have to try something different.

"The *lesson* I took away from the *campaign* was that, in the end, we had **no alternative** to armed and violent resistance. Over and over again, we had used all the **non-violent weapons** in our arsenal— speeches…threats, marches, strikes…voluntary imprisonment—all to no avail, for whatever we did was met by an *iron hand*."

Along with other groups who
were fighting for change, the
ANC formed the <u>Congress
Alliance</u>. Together, they wrote the
<u>Freedom Charter</u>—a promise to
fight for freedom and democracy
for ALL South Africans.

THE FREEDOM CHARTER

WE, THE PEOPLE OF SOUTH AFRICA,
BLACK AND WHITE, TOGETHER—
EQUALS, COUNTRYMEN,
AND BROTHERS—ADOPT THIS
FREEDOM CHARTER.

AND WE PLEDGE OURSELVES TO STRIVE
TOGETHER, SPARING NOTHING OF
OUR STRENGTH AND COURAGE, UNTIL
THE DEMOCRATIC CHANGES HERE SET
OUT HAVE BEEN WON.

1. THE PEOPLE SHALL GOVERN
2. ALL NATIONAL GROUPS SHALL HAVE EQUAL RIGHTS
3. THE PEOPLE SHALL SHARE IN THE COUNTRY'S WEALTH
4. THE LAND SHALL BE SHARED AMONG THOSE WHO WORK IT
5. ALL SHALL BE EQUAL BEFORE THE LAW
6. ALL SHALL ENJOY EQUAL HUMAN RIGHTS
7. THERE SHALL BE WORK AND SECURITY
8. THE DOORS OF LEARNING AND CULTURE SHALL BE OPENED
9. THERE SHALL BE HOUSES, SECURITY, AND COMFORT
10. THERE SHALL BE PEACE AND FRIENDSHIP

The government did not like the Freedom Charter. Just after dawn on 5 December 1956, Nelson heard a loud knocking on his door. He was arrested, along with Oliver, Walter, and 153 other leaders of the Congress Alliance and the ANC.

They were all charged with <u>high treason</u>—planning to use violence to get rid of the government.

The trial lasted more than four years. The <u>prosecution</u> could not prove that the <u>defendants</u> wanted to use violence, and in 1961 they were found not guilty.

But during the trial, something terrible happened.

NEWS

ANTI-PASS DEMONSTRATION LEADS TO BLOODSHED

69 DEAD, 180 INJURED IN RIOTS

On 21 March 1960, more than 5,000 people gathered at the police station in Sharpeville, a black township. They were protesting against a law that said black people had to carry <u>passbooks</u> whenever they traveled outside their homes—or risk 30 days in prison. They had left their passbooks at home. The protestors did not have guns, although some threw stones. The police shot at them from armored vehicles, killing 69 people.

People around the world began to criticize South Africa's apartheid laws. But the government and the police would not accept any blame. Instead they blamed the ANC and banned the whole organization.

Driver

Gardener

But Nelson and the ANC did not give up. Nelson went into hiding and became a master of disguise. Newspapers called him the Black Pimpernel after a famous character who was good at avoiding capture.

Ordinary man with a beard

Chef

The ANC decided they had no choice but to fight for freedom in a different way. Nelson sent a letter to the newspapers:

I will not leave South Africa, nor will I surrender. Only through hardship, sacrifice, and militant action can freedom be won. The struggle is my life. I will continue fighting for freedom until the end of my days.

He helped the ANC to form a secret army, known as the "Spear of the Nation." He traveled to other countries to ask for help, and trained as a soldier.

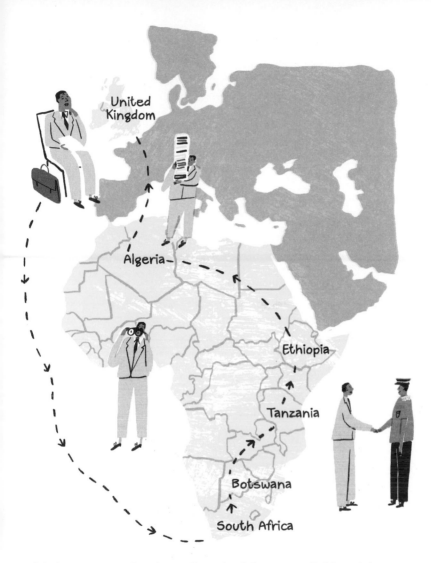

Nelson came back to South Africa in 1962, with a false passport and a new name. But soon after his return, he was stopped and arrested while he was in disguise.

Nelson and seven other men, including Walter, were accused of <u>sabotage</u> and plotting to overthrow the government. Police had discovered weapons at the headquarters of the Spear of the Nation.

If the men were found guilty, they could face the death sentence.

The trial began in October 1963. In 1964, Nelson made a famous speech from the dock. He spoke for four hours. He admitted some of the charges, but explained why he had done what he had done.

"During my lifetime I have dedicated myself to **this struggle** of the African people. I have fought against white <u>domination</u>, and I have fought against black domination. I have cherished the ideal of a democratic and **free society**...It is an ideal which I hope to live for and to achieve. But if needs be, it is an ideal for which I am **prepared to die.**"

Nelson and seven other men were found guilty. But instead of the death penalty, they were sentenced to life in prison.

Nelson was 46 years old.

Nelson was sent to South Africa's maximum-security prison on Robben Island.

His cell was tiny, with thin blankets and a bucket for a toilet. The days were spent in the courtyard, crushing stones with hammers to make gravel, working in silence.

"That small, cramped space was to be *my home* for I knew not how long."

Each day was the same as the one before. Time seemed to stand still.

To stop him losing track, Nelson began to mark a calendar on his cell wall.

At the start of his ~~sentence,~~
Nelson was allowed just one visitor
every year and one letter every six
~~months. When letters~~ did arrive,
news was scribbled or chopped out.
With no radio or newspapers, the
prisoners had little idea ~~what was~~
~~happening in the~~ outside world.

After five years in prison, Nelson got a telegram telling him his eldest son had been killed in a car crash.

"I returned to my cell and lay on my bed. I do not know how long I stayed there..."

When Nelson started his sentence,
he and the ANC thought that things
would soon change in South Africa,
and that the prisoners would be
released in a year or two.

But Nelson spent 18 years on Robben Island.

Inside prison, Nelson fought for better rights for the prisoners. Things began to improve. He was eventually allowed to set up a garden in the courtyard, growing tomatoes, chilies, and onions. It was a small taste of freedom.

Outside prison, the fight for freedom went on. Oliver Tambo ran the ANC from outside South Africa. Countries around the world began to put pressure on the South African government and to stage protests. In the 1980s, the ANC launched a new campaign.

In 1982, Nelson and Walter were moved to Pollsmoor Prison on the mainland and Nelson started a new garden on the prison roof.

Then, in 1988, the South African government started to change some of the apartheid laws. They began talking to Nelson more seriously about stopping the fighting and working together towards peace.

In December 1989, Nelson met with the new president of South Africa, F.W. de Klerk, to talk about a new South Africa. A month later, President de Klerk lifted the ban on the ANC, which meant that Nelson and the other political prisoners would soon be free!

After 27 years, Nelson walked out of prison on 11 February 1990. He was 71 years old.

He hugged his wife, children, and grandchildren. More than ten thousand days of imprisonment were over at last.

"When I was among the crowd I raised my right fist, and there was a roar. I had not been able to do that for 27 years and it gave me a surge of strength and joy."

Nelson thanked everyone around the world who had campaigned for his release. He asked all South Africans to work together towards peace.

In 1991, Nelson became leader of the ANC. He led the party in talks with President de Klerk to end apartheid, and make South Africa a true democracy.

*"If you **want to make peace** with your enemy, you have to **work with your enemy**. Then he becomes your partner."*

The government scrapped the last of the apartheid laws. In 1993, President de Klerk and Nelson shared the <u>Nobel Peace Prize</u>.

But Nelson's work was not
finished yet. On 27 April 1994, millions
of black South Africans were allowed
to vote for the first time.

The ANC won the election and Nelson Mandela
became the first president of South Africa to be
elected by ALL its people.

It was the end of Nelson's long walk to freedom, but the start of a journey to build a new South Africa. Nelson was president for five years. He worked to improve housing, schools, and life for South Africa's black people, so everyone could be equal.

Nelson died on 5 December 2013, aged 95. His story inspires people all over the world. He was an ordinary man who learned to overcome his fear and do what he felt was right. He kept going every time he fell.

Every year on 18 July, people celebrate Mandela Day. They remember the 67 years Nelson spent fighting for freedom by giving 67 minutes of their time to help others.

What will you do?

"It is what difference we have made to the lives of others that will determine the significance of the life we lead."

Timeline

1918 Rolihlahla Mandela is born on 18 July, in South Africa.

1925 Rolihlahla attends a primary school run by British missionaries. On the first day the teacher gives him an English name — Nelson.

1930 Nelson's father dies and he is placed in the care of Jongintaba Dalindyebo, the acting king of the Thembu people.

1942 Nelson attends meetings of the African National Congress (ANC), an organization fighting for a more equal society. He completes his BA.

1943 Nelson enrols for a Law Degree at Wits University.

1944 Nelson, Walter Sisulu, and Oliver Tambo set up the ANC Youth League.

Nelson marries Evelyn Mase. They have four children together.

1956 Nelson, Oliver, Walter, and 153 other leaders of the Congress Alliance and ANC are arrested. They are charged with high treason.

1958 Nelson divorces Evelyn Mase and marries Nomzano Winnie Madikizela. They have two children together.

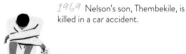

1960 On 21 March, police kill 69 people at an anti-passbook demonstration in Sharpeville.

The ANC is banned, forcing the organization into hiding.

1964 Nelson is found guilty and sentenced to life in prison. He is sent to South Africa's highest-security prison on Robben Island.

1969 Nelson's son, Thembekile, is killed in a car accident.

1982 Nelson and Walter are moved to Pollsmoor Prison on the mainland. Nelson creates a garden on the prison's roof.

1993 Nelson is awarded the Nobel Peace Prize.

1994 Millions of black South Africans vote for the first time, and Nelson is elected president of South Africa — the first to be elected by ALL its people.

2013 Nelson Mandela dies on 5 December, aged 95.

1939 Nelson enrols in a Bachelor of Arts at the University College of Fort Hare.

1940 Nelson and Oliver Tambo are expelled from university after joining student protests.

1941 Nelson decides to become a lawyer, getting a job as a clerk at a law firm in Johannesburg. He resumes his studies at the University of South Africa.

1948 The National Party comes to power and institutes apartheid, forcing white and non-white Africans to live separately.

1952 The Defiance Campaign begins.

Nelson sets up his own law firm with Oliver Tambo. It is the only South African law firm run by black lawyers!

1955 The Congress Alliance, made up of the ANC and other groups fighting for social change, issues the Freedom Charter—a promise to fight for freedom and democracy for all South Africans.

1961 Following a very long trial, the leaders of the Congress Alliance and the ANC are found not guilty!

Nelson helps form the Spear of the Nation, a secret army to fight against apartheid.

1962 After traveling internationally to raise support for their secret army, Nelson returns to South Africa in disguise, but he and seven other men are soon discovered and arrested for treason.

1963 The trial begins.

1988 The South African government begins talking to Nelson more seriously about working together towards peace.

1990 The new president of South Africa, F.W. de Klerk, lifts the ban on the ANC and releases Nelson on 11 February.

1991 Nelson becomes the leader of the ANC. He continues his fight against apartheid.

Today Nelson Mandela remains a huge source of inspiration for anyone facing inequality.

Nelson Mandela

Glossary

apartheid – meaning "apartness," apartheid was a system of laws and rules that forced black and white South Africans to live separately. Introduced by the National Party in 1948, the laws remained in place until 1991, when President F.W. de Klerk began to remove them.

African National Congress (ANC) – a political organization founded in 1912 to fight for black and mixed-race Africans' right to vote in elections. The ANC was banned from 1960 to 1990, so the party had to work secretly for many years. Nelson Mandela was elected president of the ANC in 1991.

African National Congress Youth League – a branch of the ANC formed by Nelson Mandela, Walter Sisulu, and Oliver Tambo in 1944, to involve more young people in the fight against racial inequality.

Congress Alliance – a collection of political groups that came together in the 1950s to create a fairer society. They realized that they had a much better chance of achieving their goals if they worked together. The Congress Alliance published the Freedom Charter in 1955.

Defiance Campaign – a form of peaceful protest introduced by the ANC in 1952, in which protesters risked prison by ignoring the "whites only" signs in places such as post offices, shops, and trains. Although the campaign was ultimately unsuccessful, it showed that people were willing to fight against apartheid and increased support for the ANC.

defendant – a person who has been accused of a crime and whose guilt or innocence is being decided in a court of law.

domination – to have power or control over someone or something.

Freedom Charter – a document written by the Congress Alliance in 1955 that outlined the type of country they wanted South Africa to become. Thousands of South Africans helped shape the charter by sending letters to the congress, outlining the freedoms they wanted all South Africans to have.

high treason – to betray your country by planning to use violence to get rid of a leader or government.

missionary – a member of a religious group, who is sent to a foreign country to educate others about their religion's beliefs.

Nobel Peace Prize – one of five prizes awarded each year for outstanding work in different areas, such as science, medicine, and literature.

The Nobel Prize was started by the Swedish inventor Alfred Nobel in 1895.

passbook – a document given to all black South Africans during apartheid, which said where they had the right to live, work, and travel. Black people had to carry passbooks whenever they traveled outside their homes, or risk 30 days in prison.

prosecution – the lawyers in a court case, who have to prove that the defendant is guilty.

protest – an act designed to show your unhappiness with something—often laws or leaders—in the hope that it will change.

right – the moral or legal freedom to have or to do something, such as the right to vote and have access to clean drinking water.

sabotage – to try and weaken or stop something from working on purpose. You can sabotage an object or something less concrete, such as a government.

Spear of the Nation – the ANC's secret army, set up by Nelson in 1961 to fight apartheid, once it had become clear that the government would not respond to peaceful protests.

Thembu – the South African clan that Nelson and his family belonged to. Thembu people have their own culture and traditions, and speak a language called Bantu.

township – a suburb or town in which only black South Africans were allowed to live during apartheid. Townships were usually located outside a city and often did not have the same benefits as whites-only towns and settlements.

Index

African National Congress 20, 24–25, 26, 28–29, 30, 32, 37, 38, 48, 51, 53, 56–57

African National Congress Youth League 21

Alexandra township 19

apartheid 22, 24, 26–27, 28, 37, 52, 56

British missionary school 10

Congress Alliance 30, 32

Dalindyebo, Jongintaba 12–13, 15, 17

Dalindyebo, Justice 12–13, 15, 16–17

de Klerk, F.W. 53, 56

Defiance Campaign 24–25, 29

Fanny, Nosekeni 6

Freedom Charter 30–31, 32

Gandhi, Mahatma 21

Great Place 12–13

Johannesburg 16, 18–19, 28

Mphakanyiswa, Gadla Henry 6, 11

Mqhekezweni 12, 15

Nobel Peace Prize 56

Pollsmoor Prison 52

Robben Island 44, 49

Sharpeville 35

Sisulu, Walter 18, 21, 32, 40, 52

Spear of the Nation 38, 40

Sophiatown 28

Tambo, Oliver 14–15, 21, 26, 28, 32, 51

Thembu people 6, 12–13

University of Fort Hare 14

Credits

Photograph on page 61 courtesy of Alessia Pierdomenico / Shutterstock.com

Nelson's own words are quoted from his autobiography: *Long Walk to Freedom* (Back Bay Books, New York, 1995)